The Art of Sidewalking

The Art of Sidewalking

COLE FELDMAN

The Art of Sidewalking

www.colefeldman.net

ISBN: 0-9963608-5-9
ISBN-13: 978-0-9963608-5-2

Cover designer: Sabina Kencana
Interior illustrator: Sabina Kencana
Editors: Hannah Shipp, Emma Fenton, Lake Heckaman,
Hannah Teryn, Kerry Wade, Anya Jiménez

CONTENTS

~

I. LIVING ROOM

II. KITCHEN

III. NEIGHBOR

IV. BEDROOM

V. STREET

VI. SIDEWALK

VII. PARK

VIII. BAJA

IX. BIG SKY

X. IN MY HEAD

NEVER NOTHING NOVEL

I've ascended
The same stairs
At least a hundred
Maybe a thousand
Times before
To the second floor
Unit number five
Usually looking down
At the drab carpet
Darkened by many
Monotonous steps

But today I glanced up
And got a glimpse
Of a bright light
Under an arched doorway
Glistening, golden
Shining to show me
That even amid
What masquerades
As mundane
There is always
Something new

MORE THAN ENOUGH

Louder than conversations
In the apartment next door

I hear the simple silence
Whispering to me

What if not to be
Is Shakespeare's answer

And all of this
Has become too much

A NAIL

A lone, slim
Silver nail

Protrudes

From the white wall
Where a picture frame
Used to hang

A BOOK

Fallen
From the shelf

Lying
On the carpet

Looking
Out of place

I think I should
Get off the couch

Pick up the book
And place it back

On the shelf
With the others

But then again
Maybe I should leave it
Right where it is

Because that is
Where it is
For whatever reason

And the argument
That it should be
On the shelf

Does not hold
Any more weight
In my mind

Than the argument
That things should be
Left as they are

MY NEW PINK SHIRT

My whites
Aren't as white
As they would be
If I didn't wash them
With my colors

LIKE A SHADOW LANTERN

Shining from street light
Between tree branches
And fire escape rails

Tinted by window glass
Shaped by drapes
Entering our bedroom

Making a movie for me
Wide-eyed, watching
The walls come to life

STARING AT THE WALL

If I sit
And stare
Long enough

I start to see
The space
In between

Focusing
On each speck
Of dust

Lingering
Lazily afloat
Amid light beam

Small souls
Suspended
In purgatory

On their way
Either up
Into the ether

Or down
To another life
On earth

STARING AT THE CEILING

I like to lie and look at the ordinary
With eyes as patient as rivers

Eroding through centuries
Of shallow sediment

To carve a canyon
Of deep intrigue

CEILING FAN

The fan spins so fast
It shakes its centerpiece

And the blades blur
Into a solid circle

If you spin your eyes
Around with it

You can catch a glimpse
Of a single blade

Static, for a moment
In the blur

The blade flashes
To cry, to beg

For escape
From the race

That sprints
Lap after lap

Never ending
Going nowhere

CEILING SCAR

The same section of ceiling
Shimmering in the noontime
Shows a patch of poor plastering

But perhaps on purpose
If the handyman were a sculptor
Tired of flat, featureless ceilings

So he took his trowel
Stepped up his ladder
And really went to work

To the average tenant
The depth and dimension
Might look like a blemish

As for me
I wish I could
Shake the handyman's hand

WATCHING A CANDLE BURN

A candle
Is the most civilized
Form of fire

Its occupation
Is singular

Its daily wax
Is rationed

Its lifetime
Is predefined

Its destiny
Is a straight line

Its death
Is predictable

Its dreams
Are of becoming
A wildfire

CANDLE KILLER

Screwed the lid
Onto the glass jar

While the wick
Was still burning

Watched the flame
Choke, gasp

Lose its strength
And slowly shrink

As the light
Left the room

RUBBING MY EYES IN THE SHOWER

Rubbing my eyes
Accustomed to seeing
The real world

Pressing and twisting
Wet knuckles
Into weary sockets

While forgetting
Being a body
In a shower

With eyes for legs
I chase after
Abstract patterns

Like fireflies
In the night
Behind my eyelids

A yellow halo
Pulses and blurs
Off into the distance

Stars shoot
Across my own
Internal solar system

Where I can play
Like an always
Awestruck child

At least amused
By wonders
I may never understand

MUSICAL CHAIR

I got bored of sitting
And started drumming
On the armrests

Tapping a rapid
Multi-fingered rhythm
On one arm

A deeper, bass beat
With my whole palm
On the other

Bobbing my head
Bouncing my feet
Really getting into it

TURN IT UP

"No exclamation points in poetry"
Is a rule I once read
But I'm going to break it!

Because it's been a while
Since I've gotten drunk
And danced around the room like this

The music is blaring
The windows are open wide
And I'm feeling, oh, so alive

SINGING BOWL

As I gathered bowls
From the cupboard

One clinked
Against another

And made a song
Of a single note

Resounding
In the quiet
Of the kitchen

MICROWAIT

Neon-green
Digital lines
Transform

Into the next
Number
Then the next

The seconds
Seem to last
Longer

Watching
The microwave
Count down

Waiting
For my coffee
To warm

BANANAS

A bunch ripened
All at once

I ate only one
Perfectly yellow

Those eaten early
Were too green

The others eaten late
Had brown spots

BLUEBERRIES

I got a handful of blueberries
Out of the carton

And went to wash them
But I dropped one

So I picked it up
And washed it

You wouldn't believe me
If I told you

I dropped the same blueberry
A second time

But I did
And washed it again

WASHING DISHES

In a conversation
About a meal now past

A scraped and dirty
Dinner plate

Can only say so much
With crumby words

To the sophisticated
White porcelain sink

With an acquired taste
For dishwater

SPRING

Outside our window
Stretched branches
Bare for months

When we too
Under duress of winter
Barely sustained ourselves

But now blossoming
Buds of green granting
To my bed-lying head

Hopes of spring
To get out again
And grow

BRANCHES IN THE RAIN

Branches bend
Burdened by rain

Their leaves
Dance in the wind

Dodging drops
Dripping down

From leaves
Already laden

On branches
Above

BRANCH LOVERS

One branch
Intersects
Another

I wonder if either
Longed for the other
Before they met

And if they now
Miss each other
As they grow apart

BEFORE THE FALL

I wish
The wind
Wouldn't worry

Blowing
So stressed
And serious

The leaves
Will all
Shake free

Before
The fall
Is over

BRANCH REVOLUTION

One rebel branch
Stands steady
Amid the quivering

Finally fed up
With the authoritarian
Wind regime

Refusing to pay
The gusts levied
To take its leaves

Shouts to the sky,
"We hold these trunks
To be seed-evident"

That all branches
Are free to move
Or stay still

In accordance
With the will
Of their wood

DOMESTIC BRANCH

In the morning
I found
A branch
Had grabbed hold
Of the open
Window frame
Sometime
In the night
As if
To make its way
Inside
Out of the wind

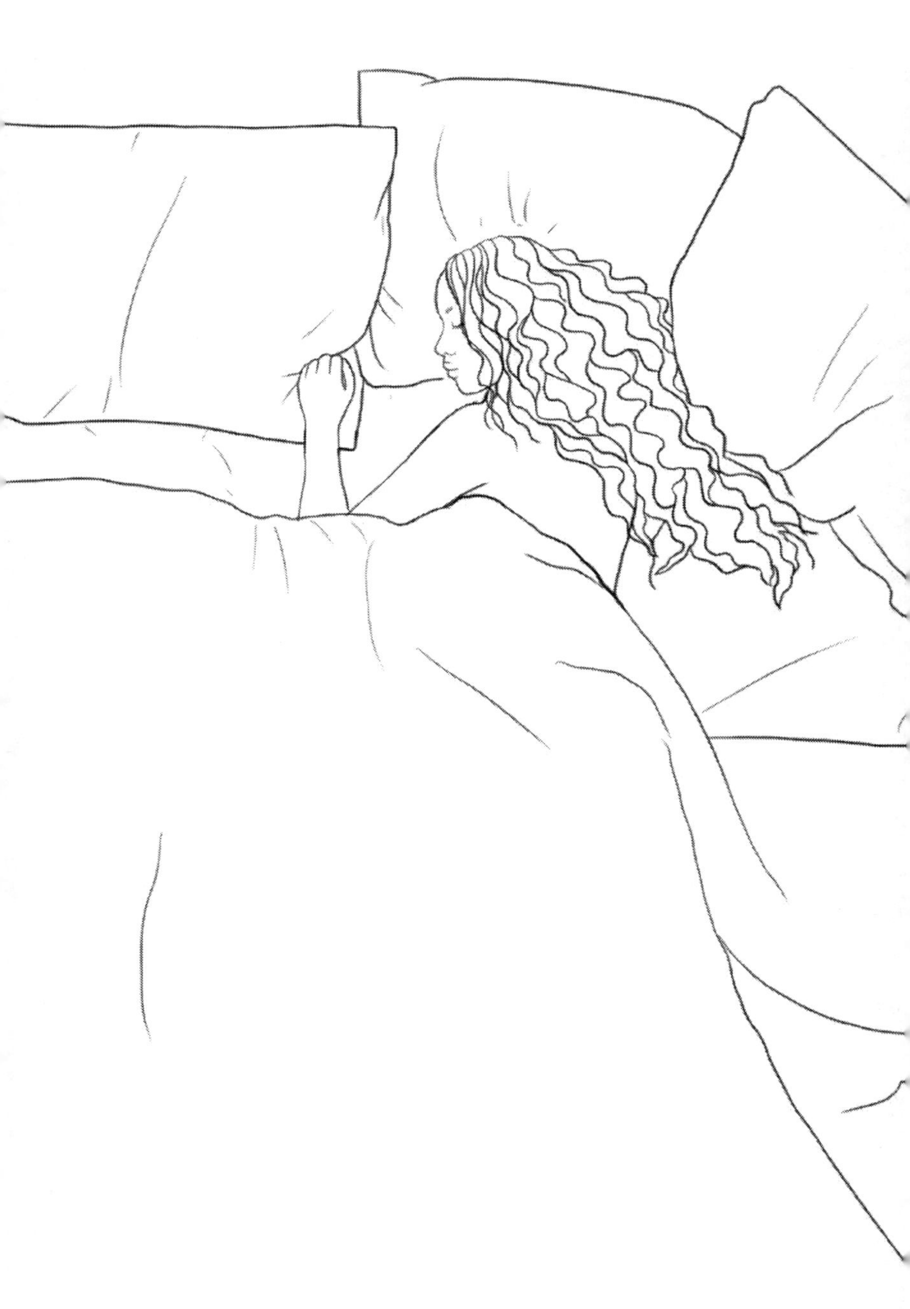

HEADS OR TAILS

It's loud with the window open
It's hot with the window closed

So we flip
                    a coin
                                        each night

Heads, let in the street noise
Tails, sweat through the sheets

RISE AND FALL

Lying down
Breathing deeply
Through my nose

With my fingers
Interlaced
Over my chest

I can feel
The rise and fall
Of it all

MIDNIGHT MASS

Lying awake listening
To the radiator wheeze
And the fridge whir
I learn as much
As I ever have
From words
Spoken with some
Supposed meaning
That I've yet to grasp

BIRDBATH BAR

A bird singing
Shrill and off-key
In the middle of the night

Must be drunk
Flying home
From the birdbath bar

CARS IN A STORM

Outside
Under eyes
Of soft storm
Slick tires
Skate across
Wet road
Wafting wind-
Carried car noise
Shooting by
Slip
Sliding along

AM RADIO

A car radio plays
At the stoplight
Outside our apartment
At 3 a.m.
And I wonder
If the driver
Is an early worker
Or a late traveler
Trying to stay awake

HER HEART

If the pulse
In my hand
On her chest
Is her heart
Or my blood
Become one
I cannot tell
Who is who
Like roots
That run deep
Into soil
Sending life
Back and forth

HER ROAR

I lay my ear
Against her skin
And hear a roar

Like listening
To the mouth
Of a seashell

And hearing
All the life
Of the ocean

Inside her sweet
Silent, sleeping
Small body

SLEEP TALKER

Up at night
I talk to myself
Until I'm hoarse

And then wonder
In the morning
If it was worth it

Because I can't remember
A single thing
I said

SLEEP SCIENCE

Lying in bed
Cold at first
Added a blanket

Then got hot
Pushed the blanket
Halfway down

Then cold again
Brought the blanket
Back up a quarter

Eventually got up
To find a thermometer
And a ruler

COMFORTABLE ENOUGH

I lay in bed
And thought

If I move this
That way

Or bend that
This way

Then I might be
More comfortable

But ended up
Lying still

And falling asleep
As I was

CREAKY FLOOR

I've learned which boards
Creak in the floor

When I wake in the night
For a drink of water

But I walk over them anyway
Too tired to care

CITY ALARM

Birds sing
Their wake-up song
Through the window crack

Car wheels
Screech to a stop
At the traffic light

Road workers
Beep their backhoes
And jack their hammers

She breathes
In bed beside me
A deep, waking sigh

I stretch and roll over
To see the sun
Has yet to rise

But another day
In the city
Has already begun

LAZY MORNING

Lazy
Like the dewfall

Doing nothing
In the morning

Except lying
On leafy sheets

DREAM DIRT

A daytime nap
Marries the motion
And light
Of the waking world
With the wonder
And formlessness
Of dream
Where poetry lives
In the middle
Dancing
Back and forth
In wheelbarrows
Full of dream dirt
Dug up in sleep
And delivered
To be replanted
Here in bed
Where my words
First take root

NAPTIME

Noontime sun
Seeps in

Singing of searching
Clouded and loud

For thunder could not
Strike so straight

Turned away by light
Things, bright things

Searching still
In this dark, draped bedroom

Go back now light
Whence you came

You will find naught
But darkness here

NAP TRAP

I woke up wobbly
Without my brain

Late
For a dinner date

Snatched my coat
And stumbled

Down the stairs
To catch the bus

Paid my fare
And sat confused

By being back
In the real world

So suddenly
After dreaming

WRITING IN THE CITY #1

Through the open
Emergency exit
On the bus

I watched
Where the buildings
Scraped the sky

And I knew
There was something
About that border

Built between
Our working world
And the heavens

But I couldn't
In the moment
Muster the words

I rode the same route
For weeks
And wrote nothing

Until the clouds
Picked up a spire
Like a spear

And stabbed
Through the hatch
Into my heart

Only then, bleeding
Did I have ink
To dip my pen

So I could write
What escaped me
Bus rides before

WRITING IN THE CITY #2

I stop anywhere
To write

On the street corner
In the rain

On my phone
On the bus

In conversation
On the move

Anytime
I'm in the mood

It comes to me
Only so often

I can't afford
To let it go

SELFISH

Sitting
In the backseat
Thinking
Of my own problems

I realize
The driver
Is patting his knee
Impatiently

And must also
Have things
Other than driving
To do

RUSH HOUR

There's this deep
Urban gorge
Between buildings

Filled with yellow-
Headlight fish
Swimming upstream

I can see from here
On the hilltop
In the suburbs

The river of light
Pinching into the distance
Downtown

SUBURBIA

In a circle of bikes
On a side street
In suburban San Francisco

The kids are wary
About what they say
While grown-ups stand by

They cover their mouths
And tell secrets to their friends

About what they watched on TV
When their parents weren't around

DRUNK TRUCK

The trash truck
Raises its arm

Shaking the bin
Like a drinker

Leaning back
With a glass

Thirsting
For the last drop

IMPOSTOR

On the bus
Blending in

With the up-for-work
Commuter crowd

Pretending
I slept last night

When I was really
In the warehouse

With my eyes closed
Worshipping

In a different
Congregation

Wondering whether
I could call in sick

But alas, here I am
Holding the handrail

Headed to the office
Like a non-believer

WRITING IN THE CITY #3

The wheel
Of a mail truck

Pulls up
And over
The curb

Becomes
A moment
Unto itself

Another car honks
A cyclist shouts

I could return
To the wheel
And the curb

But other
Interruptions

Pigeons
And sirens

Come one
After another

So I can't remember
What the moment
Was before

And it changes
All the time

WRITING IN THE CITY #4

I start a poem
While walking

Trying to remember
The first few lines

Repeating them
Over and over

Until I can find
A place to write

Another line
Comes to mind

Four now
Repeating them

And a fifth
Still a ways away

At risk of forgetting
The beginning

To remember
The end

FASHION SHOW

The white building
Is orange this morning

Wearing the red stoplight
And the rising yellow sun

ROCKING CHAIR

On the patio
Outside the cafe

A wicker chair
With four legs

Has two legs
Slightly shorter

So it rocks
Side to side
In the wind

CITY SYMPHONY

A songbird
Sings soprano

A car horn
Beeps baritone

—Slightly
More symphonic

Than the city sounds
I am used to

A DEAD BIRD

On the sidewalk
Once flying
Now lying
Dead
So very dead

DARK DAY

A black crow
Perched
On a black power line

With black
Clouds behind
Bodes ill, I fear

As if the day
Were not already
Dark enough

YOUR NAME

I hear your name called
At a coffee shop
By the barista

Waiting for someone else
Who is not you
To pick up their order

Can't possibly be you
I know that

But I still can't resist
Turning around

PEOPLE STORE

At the grocery store
I peruse the aisles
And pretend

The paper boxes
And packages
Are people

With labels listing
Their ingredients
And health facts

What a way
That would be
To shop for

Falafel friends
Linguini lovers
Edamame enemies

All part
Of a balanced
Social diet

A YOUNG MAN

Slouched against
A fire hydrant
With his feet
On the street

Right hand
Holding left forearm
Left hand
Holding a cigarette

Smoking
Chewing gum
And looking up
At the building tops

AN OLD MAN

At a restaurant
Hunched over the table
Using a magnifying glass
To read the menu

A JAYWALKER

Walks across
The crosswalk

Ignoring
The red hand

Telling him
To wait

HAT HANDLER

A man sits
On a brick bench

With his elbows
On his knees

Leaning forward
Looking

At the ground
Rocking

Back and forth
Holding

An upturned hat
By the brim

Shaking it
For money

TOGETHER

Across the street
A crowd stands
Huddled together
Underneath
An overhang
In the rain

WHAT A HUMAN CAN DO

We bend ourselves
Into shapes

I wonder
What a human

Can do
With some space

THAT'S NOT ALL

When I walk
From downtown
Out to the coast
To see the water

—And the horizon—

I remember
There is more
And I am small
And it's alright

TRANSPLANTED

In square-foot
Sections of sidewalk
Stand the survivors

Stumps of their ancestors
Have long since
Been cemented over

Surrounded by buildings
And streets that don't speak
The same language

Drinking sewer water
Eating artificial light
Breathing engine exhaust

Some couples
Are close enough
To hold branches

Together they dream
Of raising saplings
In a park

TAG

The kids
Chasing each other
In the park

Have no idea
The game they play
Is primal

Our ancestors
Played the same game

And tore apart
The loser
With their teeth

—Nowadays
We chase and catch
But don't devour

And it's all
Just a game

THE SHOOTER

Brought a ball
Inside a backpack
To the court
In the park

Set his bag
On a bench
Unzipped
Took out the ball

Dribbled
To the line
Looked up
At the backboard

Just before sunset
I watched him
Bend his knees
And shoot

A PHOTOGRAPHER

Stood in the shade
Resting the lens
On his leg

Like a hunter
Waiting to shoot
A bird in the trees

He waited
Still as a cat

Only moving
His other arm

To take drags
On his cigarette

KITE-CATCHERS

They call these trees
In the park
With more kites
Than leaves

BUTTERFLY

A falling leaf
No, a butterfly

Moved about
More by

The whims
Of the wind

Than the will
Of its wings

WE ARE NOT BIRDS!

The plane bumps
But we are safe
I guess
Based on how calm
Everyone is
Sitting in their seats
Carrying on
Their conversations
As though
There were more
Than empty air
Between us
And the mountains
Down below

HOW FAR WE'VE COME

We didn't even
Have plumbing
In buildings
On the *ground*

And now
We have toilets
In *planes*
That flush!

AT THE VILLA

We sat and listened
To the wives
Talk about how
They prefer to fly
First class

As the fountain splashed
Into the private pool
In the background

We nodded and pretended
(As grateful guests do)
That we lived similar lives
And could understand
When they said

Flying economy
Was completely
Out of the question

COOL WAR

Lounging
In a beach chair

I point and shoot
My finger gun

At boats
Out on the water

Making war
In peacetime

UP ABOVE

I wonder what's
On the backs of clouds

If they carry sky people
Across the blue

I only see bellies
Full and fluffy
From down below

BLUE DAY

The clouds dissipate
The line between
Ocean and sky
Evaporates, and
The two blue worlds
Become one

SAILOR'S STORY

Back at the beach
Unable to keep
Boredom at bay

Left behind
And sailed away

Seeking stories
To match the sailor's
In the barroom

Boisterous
And spilling his beer

Is as close
To drowning
As he's ever been

MEXICAN BEER

From the lime seed
Floundering
At the bottom
Of the bottle

A pillar of bubbles
Ascend to escape
An amber ocean
Of intoxication

I grab the neck
Suck some down
And sink to suffer
With the seed

SAN JOSÉ PIANIST

Hunched over
So close to the keys
He could kiss them

Leaning back
He almost fell
Out of his chair

Swinging his head
Side to side
Hair in his eyes

Fingers jumping
From key to key
Like grasshoppers

Taking off and landing
On notes of pressed
And held passion

I don't know
Much about music

But I can feel
When someone is feeling it

And I could feel him
Feeling himself

And everyone else there
Was feeling him too

CABO DRUMMER

He asked if I liked music
I said yes
He asked if I played an instrument
I said no

I wanted to say more
But my Spanish was *muy mal*
And his English was just good enough
To ask me those two questions

So we shared a brief
Mostly-wordless moment
Outside the taqueria
Where his band played

He leaned against the wall
Waiting to go back on
Swigging from his beer
And puffing on his cigarette

Seemingly unaware
Of just how
Archetypically himself
He was being

While I stood by, watching
With my hands in my pockets
Feeling much less talented
Than the man I was admiring

TODOS SANTOS SHOP OWNER

Said she grew up
In San Clemente

The only people there
Were jarheads and surfers

One day
Her mom asked,

"Why don't you bring home
A nice marine

Instead of all
These surfer boys?"

NIGHT CLUB

A single boat
Bobs amorously
Out on the water

Showing off
In a shaft
Of moonlight

She knows
All the hotels
Are watching

With folded arms
They stand
On dry land

The lights
In their windows
Wink on and off

They lean in the wind
Looking side to side
Along the coast

Waiting to see
Which one of them
Will be first

To step out
Onto the dance floor
Of the night

SHY STAR

I arrived early
For the sunrise show

Took my seat
On the deck

And waited
In the dark

For the cloud curtains
To part

But the mountain stage
Remained empty

While the star
Hid below the horizon

Like a shy child
Who forgets every night

He is the sun god
And must muster again

The courage
To shine

TIGHT ROPE

A single thread
Of spider web
S t r e t c h e d
From the table
To the ottoman

With a dewdrop
Weighing it down
In the center

A spider
Must have made
The leap
Across the chasm
In the night

LYING ON THE DECK IN THE SUN

Eyes closed, I imagined
There were at least
Three layers

Sun
Legs
And couch cushions

But I couldn't distinguish
The beams beating
The skin of my shins

From the pillows
Pressing up against
My calf muscles

An amalgamation
Of warmth from the rays
Comfort from the cushions

And my inferior appendages
Somewhere, sensing
The warmth and the comfort

I knew that
My legs rested
On top of the cushions

And the sun
Somehow
Warmed them

But when I looked
For my lower limbs
In my mind

There was only the mass
Into which the three layers
Had melded

A ROBIN

Flew up
And perched
Atop a fir tree

Twittering softly
Twitching its tail feathers
Erratically flapping its wings

I could see the bird clearly
In contrast
To the monochrome sky

I looked down to write
But when I looked back
The robin was gone

THE WIND AND THE LIGHT

I didn't know
I was barging in
On an orgy

When I opened the door
To the guest room
Where I slept last night

The cold wind blew
Through the window
I cracked to stay cool

The red curtains wavered
And rays of warm light
Drifted through the dark

It was the chill
Of the brisk morning air
Crisp in my nostrils

The way the light
Coursed through the curtains
Briefly blown open

Like a yellow brook
Between red banks
Borders burning orange

And then darkness again
When the breeze subsided
And the curtains returned

I stood in the doorway
And watched all the love
Being made without me

I guess I've got this misconception
That things are only happening
When I'm around

But the wind and the light
Lost their egos
Long ago

They play
With or without
An audience

MOUNTAIN MAN

He opened the door
To the deck

Stepped out
Onto the wood

Looked up
At the mountains

Bowed his head
And ambled forward

Humbly approaching
Their majesty

SKY HUNGER

Watching cumulus clouds
Crown the mountains

Smells from the grill
Draw eyes back inward

Down through the gut
Into pangs of hunger

More persistent
Than perceptions of beauty

To be seen
But not eaten

DRENCH WARFARE

The deck planks
Took fire
From the rain
And bled
Spreading
Wet darkness
From the bullet holes

GETTING HERE

I set out
To get here

Not really knowing
Where I was going

But now
That I've arrived
I realize

This is where
I was headed
All along

I SEE NOW

How these things
Can happen

Having seen
What I hadn't

When I wondered
How they could

HEAD SPACE

I know things now
But I fear to forget
So I write them, recite them
Read them over and over
And carry a head on my shoulders
Full of the past
Like a traveler's trunk
With too many things from home
On a journey to a place
From which there is no return
Back to how
Things were before

WISHING

I wish for what
Would require me
To read the dictionary
Cover to cover

To learn what others
Have done before me
From various
Secondary sources

And then rinse out
Their individuality
And repeat
As my own

Why can not
Wishing alone
Be enough
To muster the matter

If I were to just
Lie here in bed
Wishing hard
And sincerely

FIELD OF TIME

Perilous
Would pause be

For a picker
In the field of time

With only
A moment's harvest

And eternal drought
Thereafter

PINBALL

I bounce
From thing
To thing
Like a pinball
In between
Believing
It must be this
No, then this
Back and forth
Until my hands
Start to shake
My back aches
And I'm all
Out of chances
So I guess
I'll soon settle
Somewhere
Deep down
In the machine

HIGHS AND LOWS #1

Just as I am sure
It's all gone forever

It returns, reviving me
To go back on high

And then soon
Low once more

With less hope
Than before

That the revival
Will come again

Until it does
And I resume flight

Though I know
And of this, I am certain

There is one low
In which I will lie for good

HIGHS AND LOWS #2

Now that I've felt
The lows that lurk
Among the clouds

Lying in wait
With their anchors
To sink my soaring ship

I mistrust my highs
Interrogate their intentions
Even skip some altogether

Say no to parties
Stay out of love affairs
So I can stick in the middle

Where at least
I won't have to worry
About falling too far

WORRY

As much as I worry
There are still worries
That I haven't worried about
And I worry
About that too

THE THINKER

You seem to think
You need to think
All the time
Thinking man
Think as you can
But you just can't
Think it all

LYING TO YOURSELF

That's just not true
What you heard once
And repeated to yourself

And at some point
Started to believe
From the repeating

Having forgotten
That the original
Was a lie

Until a collision
With what's real
Reminds you

MONOTONOISE

If I sing
The same song
For too long
It starts to sound
Like silence

The same song
For too long
It starts to sound
Like silence

For too long
It starts to sound
Like silence

It starts to sound
Like silence

Like silence

WHATEVER WAXES

I recklessly write
What comes at night

Waking lately
Makes me wobble

Whatever waxes
Wanes tomorrow

Made in the USA
Columbia, SC
03 October 2021

46263436R10081